P9-CFO-783

AWESOME GOOD CLEAN

Jokes FOR KiDS

BOB PHILLIPS

HARVEST HOUSE PUBLISHERS
Eugene, Oregon 97402

AWESOME GOOD CLEAN JOKES FOR KIDS

Copyright © 1992 by Harvest House Publishers
Eugene, Oregon 97402

Phillips, Bob, 1940—
    Awesome good clean jokes for kids / Bob Phillips.
        Summary: A collection of jokes, grouped into such cate-
        gories as "School Daze," "Hoarse Laughs," and Silly
        Dillies."
    ISBN: 1-56507-062-3
    1. Wit and humor, Juvenile.   2. American wit and
        humor. [1. Jokes.] I. Title.
    PN6163.P478 1992
    818'.5402—dc20

91-12109
CIP
AC

All rights reserved. No part of this publication may be repro-
duced, stored in a retrieval system, or transmitted in any form
or by any means—electronic, mechanical, digital, photocopy,
recording, or any other—except for brief quotations in printed
reviews, without the prior permission of the publisher.

Printed in the United States of America

03 04 05 / BC / 28 27 26 25 24

*This book is dedicated to all kids
(regardless of their age)
who love to smile...laugh...and even
groan at some of these crazy jokes.
It is also dedicated to many of my friends
whose names are in
this book at various spots.*

—— & ——

*If you read any of the jokes and don't think that
they are funny...remember that humor is in
the mind of the beholder.
May everyone laugh with you
instead of at you!*

Bob Phillips
Fresno, California

About the Author

BOB PHILLIPS...is the author of over 20 books with sales reaching 3,000,000 copies in print. He is a California State Licensed Marriage, Family, and Child Counselor. Bob received his bachelor's degree from Biola University, master's degree from Cal State University in Fresno, and his Ph.D. in counseling from Trinity Seminary. He is presently the Executive Director of Hume Lake Christian Camps, one of America's largest youth and adult camping programs.

Table of Contents

Levi & Jean

Levi: What did the bee say to the rose?
Jean: I have no clue.
Levi: Hi, bud!

— & —

Levi: What do you call a man who gets walked all over?
Jean: I don't know.
Levi: Matt.

— & —

Levi: What do you get if you cross a shark with a parrot?
Jean: I have no idea.
Levi: An animal that talks your head off.

Levi: What do liars do when they die?
Jean: I give up.
Levi: Lie still.

— & —

Levi: What did the dog say when he sat on the sandpaper?
Jean: Who knows?
Levi: Ruff, ruff.

— & —

Levi: What is the difference between a mouse and a beautiful girl?
Jean: You've got me.
Levi: The mouse harms the cheese, and the girl charms the he's.

— & —

Levi: What kind of animal tells lies?
Jean: That's a mystery.
Levi: An amphibian.

— & —

Levi: What people are like the end of a book?
Jean: I'm blank.
Levi: The Finnish.

Levi: What people do the most traveling?
Jean: I don't have the foggiest.
Levi: Romans.

——— & ———

Levi: What is the right kind of timber for castles in the air?
Jean: It's unknown to me.
Levi: Sunbeams.

——— & ———

Levi: What goes through a door but never goes in or out?
Jean: I'm in the dark.
Levi: A keyhole.

——— & ———

Levi: What can go over the water and through the water without getting wet?
Jean: Search me.
Levi: Sunlight.

——— & ———

Levi: What time of day can you spell the same backward and forward?
Jean: You've got me guessing.
Levi: Noon.

Levi: What city is a small stone?
Jean: I pass.
Levi: Little Rock.

—— & ——

Levi: What is horse sense?
Jean: How should I know?
Levi: Just stable thinking.

—— & ——

Levi: What kind of policeman enjoys his work most?
Jean: I don't know.
Levi: A traffic policeman, because he whistles while he works.

2

Hubert & Erastus

Hubert: What's the highest building in New York City?
Erastus: I have no clue.
Hubert: The library. It has the most stories.

— & —

Hubert: What has four legs and feathers?
Erastus: I don't know.
Hubert: A featherbed.

— & —

Hubert: What do mice do in the daytime?
Erastus: Beats me.
Hubert: Mousework.

Hubert: What did the beaver say to the tree?
Erastus: I can't guess.
Hubert: It was nice gnawing you.

—— & ——

Hubert: What can you serve but not eat?
Erastus: I have no idea.
Hubert: A tennis ball.

—— & ——

Hubert: What musical notes do you need to walk across the ice?
Erastus: You tell me.
Hubert: C-sharp or B-flat (see sharp or be flat).

—— & ——

Hubert: What pet is found in most cars?
Erastus: I give up.
Hubert: A car-pet.

—— & ——

Hubert: What contains more feet in winter than in summer?
Erastus: Who knows.
Hubert: A skating rink.

Hubert: What are the hardest kind of beans to raise on a farm?

Erastus: You've got me.

Hubert: Jelly beans.

—— & ——

Hubert: What time did the Chinese scholar go to the dentist?

Erastus: My mind is a blank.

Hubert: 2:30 (tooth hurty).

—— & ——

Hubert: Why is it bad to look at Niagara Falls too long?

Erastus: That's a mystery.

Hubert: You may get a cataract in your eye.

—— & ——

Hubert: What is the difference between a tuna fish and a piano?

Erastus: I don't have the foggiest.

Hubert: You can't tune a fish.

—— & ——

Hubert: What goes up white and comes down yellow and white?

Erastus: It's unknown to me.

Hubert: An egg when you toss it in the air.

Hubert: What happened when the boardinghouse blew up?
Erastus: I'm in the dark.
Hubert: Roomers were flying.

— & —

Hubert: What is dark underneath, white on top, and very warm in hot weather?
Erastus: Search me.
Hubert: A wolf in sheep's clothing.

— & —

Hubert: What is a kitten after it is three days old?
Erastus: You've got me guessing.
Hubert: Four days old.

— & —

Hubert: What did the duckling say when he saw his first colored Easter egg?
Erastus: I pass.
Hubert: Ooh, look at the orange marmalade.

— & —

Hubert: What did one pile of sand say to the other?
Erastus: How should I know?
Hubert: Whatcha dune tonight?

Hubert: What do you call a very small billy goat?
Erastus: I don't know.
Hubert: A peanut butter.

3

Who's There?

Knock, knock.
Who's there?
Zoom.
Zoom who?
Zoom did you expect?

— & —

Knock, knock.
Who's there?
Megan.
Megan who?
Megan end to these knock-knock jokes,
before I knock-knock you!

Knock, knock.
Who's there?
Ether.
Ether who?
Ether Bunny.

— & —

Knock, knock.
Who's there?
Estelle.
Estelle who?
Estelle more Ether Bunnies.

— & —

Knock, knock.
Who's there?
Samoa.
Samoa who?
Samoa Ether Bunnies.

— & —

Knock, knock.
Who's there?
Consumption.
Consumption who?
**CONSUMPTION BE DONE ABOUT
ALL THESE ETHER BUNNIES?**

Knock, knock.
Who's there?
Hamen.
Hamen who?
Hamen eggs.

— & —

Knock, knock.
Who's there?
Just a minute, and I'll see.

— & —

Knock, knock.
Who's there?
Yul.
Yul who?
Yul never know.

— & —

Knock, knock.
Who's there?
Hop.
Hop who?
Hop, hop away. Ether Bunny gone!

4

The Answer Man

Q: Why should opera singers be good sailors?
A: They know how to handle high C's.

— *&* —

Q: Why is a stout man apt to be melancholy?
A: Because he is a man of size (sighs).

— *&* —

Q: Why are there no psychiatrists for dogs?
A: Everyone knows dogs aren't allowed on couches.

— *&* —

Q: Why did Jack and Jill tumble down the hill?
A: It beats walking.

Q: Why did the little girl put her father in the fridge?
A: She wanted ice cold pop.

— & —

Q: Why did Mickey Mouse go into space?
A: To find Pluto.

— & —

Q: Why don't robots panic?
A: Because they have nerves of steel.

— & —

Q: Why did the farmer wear only one boot when he went into town?
A: Because he heard there was a 50 percent chance of snow.

— & —

Q: Why did the brilliant scientist disconnect his doorbell?
A: He wanted to win the Nobel Prize.

— & —

Q: Why did the old farmer run a steam roller over his potato field?
A: He wanted to raise mashed potatoes.

Q: Why did the spy spray his room with insect repellent?
A: Because he thought it was bugged.

— & —

Q: Why does an artist lie down when he paints?
A: Because he works from his pallet.

— & —

Q: Why did Miss Muffet need a road map?
A: Because she lost her whey!

— & —

Q: Why does the Statue of Liberty stand in New York?
A: Because it can't sit!

— & —

Q: Why does a baby duck walk softly?
A: Because it can't walk hardly.

— & —

Q: Why is a dog's tail like the heart of a tree?
A: Because it is farthest from the bark.

Q: Why is a pencil like a riddle?
A: It's no good without a point.

— & —

Q: Why is a pig's tail like getting up at 4:40 A.M.?
A: It's twirly (too early).

— & —

Q: Why is your nose in the middle of your face?
A: Because it is the scenter.

— & —

Q: Why is a son at college like an electrician?
A: Because they both wire constantly for money.

— & —

Q: Why don't candle trimmers work from Monday through Friday?
A: Because they just work on wick ends.

— & —

Q: Why does a tiger kneel before it springs?
A: Because it is preying.

5

Barnaby & Basil

Barnaby: What part of a fish weighs the most?
Basil: I have no clue.
Barnaby: The scales.

—— *&* ——

Barnaby: What is the best thing to take when you are run down?
Basil: I don't know.
Barnaby: The number of the car that hit you.

—— *&* ——

Barnaby: What's the difference between a cloud on a rainy day and a boy who is being spanked?
Basil: Beats me.
Barnaby: One pours out rain and the other roars out pain.

Barnaby: What is the most disagreeable month for soldiers?
Basil: I can't guess.
Barnaby: A long March.

—— & ——

Barnaby: What did the sign on the Space Control Center's door say?
Basil: I have no idea.
Barnaby: Gone to Launch.

—— & ——

Barnaby: What spins but never seems to move?
Basil: You tell me.
Barnaby: The earth.

—— & ——

Barnaby: What's a cross between a dog and a chicken?
Basil: I give up.
Barnaby: A pooched egg.

—— & ——

Barnaby: What does a 500-pound mouse say?
Basil: Who knows?
Barnaby: Here kitty, here kitty.

Barnaby: What are the most difficult ships to conquer?
Basil: You've got me.
Barnaby: Hardships.

—— & ——

Barnaby: What goes ha, ha, ha, plop!
Basil: My mind is a blank.
Barnaby: Someone laughing his head off.

—— & ——

Barnaby: What happens when an owl has laryngitis?
Basil: I'm blank.
Barnaby: He doesn't give a hoot.

—— & ——

Barnaby: What two bows can every girl have near her hand?
Basil: I don't have the foggiest.
Barnaby: Elbows.

—— & ——

Barnaby: What did the raisin say to the coffee cake?
Basil: It's unknown to me.
Barnaby: I feel as if I'm rolling in dough.

Barnaby: What did the cow say to the pig?
Basil: I'm in the dark.
Barnaby: I'm afraid you are just a boar.

—— & ——

Barnaby: What's the spiciest animal known?
Basil: Search me.
Barnaby: A curried horse.

—— & ——

Barnaby: What did the punching bag say to the package wrapper at the sporting-goods store?
Basil: You've got me guessing.
Barnaby: Box 'em.

—— & ——

Barnaby: What kind of flour do they use to make Lassie's dog biscuits?
Basil: I pass.
Barnaby: Collie flour.

—— & ——

Barnaby: What kind of man starts at the top and ends up at the bottom?
Basil: How should I know?
Barnaby: A paper hanger.

—— & ——

Barnaby: What do you call a train carrying a load of apples and bananas?

Basil: I don't know.
Barnaby: A tooty fruity.

—— & ——

Barnaby: What kind of ears does a train have?
Basil: I don't know.
Barnaby: Engineers.

6

Knee Slappers

First peasant: I hear the dictator is going to charge us a tax every time we use our thumbs.

Second peasant: That is horrible!

First peasant: And if we don't pay, he's going to hang us!

Second peasant: We must revolt. After all, who ever heard of using thumb tax to hang people?

— & —

Mom: What did you do at school today?

Ethan: We did a guessing game.

Mom: But I thought you were having a math exam?

Ethan: That's right...

— & —

Q: What did the window say?

A: Take pains.

Q: What did a piece of ice say?
A: Keep cool.

— & —

Q: What did the calendar say?
A: Be up to date.

— & —

Q: What did the pencil say?
A: Never be led.

— & —

Q: What did the pin say?
A: Keep your head on.

— & —

Q: What did the knife say?
A: Be sharp.

— & —

Q: What did the fire say?
A: Make light around you.

— & —

Q: What did the glue say?
A: Stick to it.

Q: What did the lamp say?
A: Be bright.

— & —

Q: An apple, an orange, and a banana were sitting in a tree. The apple and orange jumped off but not the banana. Why?
A: Because he was yellow.

— & —

Shelly: Are there any colors you can actually touch?
Chuck: Oh, yes, I've often felt blue.

— & —

Did you hear about the preacher who came along and wrote on the signboard: I pray for all. Or about the lawyer who wrote underneath the preacher: I plead for all. Or the doctor who added: I prescribe for all. The one I remember the most is the plain citizen who wrote: I pay for all!

— & —

Did you hear about the young boy selling lemonade from two bowls on the same stand? In front of one bowl was a sign: Five cents a glass. In front of a second bowl was a sign: Two cents a glass.

An old gentleman stopped, looked at the signs, and bought a glass of lemonade at two cents. He smacked his lips and ordered another.

When he had finished, he asked the young boy how he expected to sell any lemonade at five cents when he was offering such a good drink for two cents.

The young boy began to explain his story. He told the old gentleman that his cat fell in the two-cent bowl about 15 minutes ago, so he thought he'd better sell it out fast before the news spread too far.

—— & ——

Hazel: Did you leave a tip for the boy who delivers our newspaper all year?

Herbert: Yes, dear. I put some of it in the bushes, some of it on the roof, and the rest of it in the front yard.

—— & ——

Chopper: I think that my mom plans to straighten up my room once and for all.

Rusty: Why do you say that?

Chopper: Because she's learning how to drive a bulldozer.

—— & ——

Austin: If you don't marry me, I'll hang myself from that tree in your front yard.

Tamara: Please don't do that. You know my parents don't want you hanging around here.

Mrs. Poure: My daughter is at the university. She's very bright, you know. Every time we get a letter from her we have to go to the dictionary.

Mrs. Phillips: You're lucky—every time we hear from our daughter we have to go to the bank.

—— & ——

Taylor: It is a little known fact that many lighthouse keepers raise hens.

Dillen: Why would they raise hens of all things?

Taylor: Apparently they like to have eggs with their beacon.

7

Priscilla & Rufus

Priscilla: What walks over the water and under the water, yet does not touch the water?

Rufus: I have no clue.

Priscilla: A woman crossing a bridge over a river with a pail of water on her head.

— & —

Priscilla: What four letters of the alphabet would scare off a burglar?

Rufus: I don't know.

Priscilla: O, I C U (Oh, I see you).

— & —

Priscilla: What do you call a sheep that has just been sheared?

Rufus: Beats me.
Priscilla: Bare, bare, black sheep.

— & —

Priscilla: What can you hold in your right hand that you can't hold in your left hand?
Rufus: I can't guess.
Priscilla: Your left elbow.

— & —

Priscilla: What do you write on a robot's gravestone?
Rufus: I have no idea.
Priscilla: Rust in piece.

— & —

Priscilla: What kind of party do prisoners like most of all?
Rufus: You tell me.
Priscilla: A going-away party.

— & —

Priscilla: What does the sun do when it sets?
Rufus: I give up.
Priscilla: Makes a night of it.

Priscilla: What is a very hair-raising experience?
Rufus: Who knows?
Priscilla: Visiting a rabbit farm.

—— & ——

Priscilla: What sits on the bottom of the ocean and shakes?
Rufus: You've got me.
Priscilla: A nervous wreck.

—— & ——

Priscilla: What do hill people use to cook their meals on?
Rufus: My mind is a blank.
Priscilla: A mountain range.

—— & ——

Priscilla: What would you call the life story of a car?
Rufus: That's a mystery.
Priscilla: An autobiography.

—— & ——

Priscilla: What makes a pair of shoes?
Rufus: I'm blank.
Priscilla: Two shoes.

Priscilla: What is the end of everything?
Rufus: I don't have the foggiest.
Priscilla: The letter G.

—— & ——

Priscilla: What do you get if you cross a cocker spaniel, a poodle, and a rooster?
Rufus: It's unknown to me.
Priscilla: A cockapoodledoo.

—— & ——

Priscilla: What's behind the stars?
Rufus: I'm in the dark.
Priscilla: Policemen.

—— & ——

Priscilla: What do they call the cabs lined up at the railroad terminal?
Rufus: Search me.
Priscilla: The yellow rows of taxis (Texas).

—— & ——

Priscilla: What did the mother say when she learned that her son had eaten 37 pancakes at one sitting?
Rufus: You've got me guessing.
Priscilla: How waffle!

Priscilla: What did King Arthur wear to bed?
Rufus: I pass.
Priscilla: A knight gown.

—— & ——

Priscilla: What did the man put on his car when the weather turned cold?
Rufus: How should I know?
Priscilla: An extra muffler.

—— & ——

Priscilla: What does an astronaut do when he gets angry?
Rufus: I don't know.
Priscilla: He blasts off.

8

Elephant Watch

Q: What did Tarzan say when he saw the elephants coming with sunglasses on?
A: Nothing. He didn't recognize them.

— & —

Q: Why do elephants' tusks stick out?
A: Because their parents couldn't afford braces.

— & —

Q: What do you do with old bowling balls?
A: Give them to the elephants to shoot at marbles.

— & —

Q: Why does an elephant have wrinkled knees?
A: From playing marbles

Q: What weighs four thousand pounds and sings?
A: Harry Elefonte.

—— & ——

Q: Why does an elephant have cracks between his toes?
A: To carry his library card.

—— & ——

Q: Why do elephants have wrinkled ankles?
A: They lace their sneakers too tightly.

—— & ——

Q: What's the difference between a loaf of bread and an elephant?
A: Well, if you don't know the difference, I'm certainly not going to send you to the store for a loaf of bread.

—— & ——

Q: Why did the elephant paint his toenails different colors?
A: So he could hide in a jellybean bag.

—— & ——

Q: What's the difference between an elephant and an orange?
A: They are different colors.

Q: What is red, blue, white, and orange?
A: A plaid elephant.

—— & ——

Q: Why did the elephant walk on two legs?
A: To give the ants a chance.

—— & ——

Q: What did one elephant say to the other?
A: Nothing. Elephants can't talk!

—— & ——

Q: Why does an elephant have red toenails?
A: So he can hide in a cherry tree.

—— & ——

Q: Why do elephants roll down the hill?
A: Because they can't roll up it very well!

—— & ——

Q: How do you get an elephant out of a box of Jell-O?
A: Follow the directions on the back of the package.

—— & ——

Q: How do you make a statue of an elephant?
A: Get a stone and carve away everything that doesn't look like an elephant.

Q: What's the difference between an elephant and a flea?

A: An elephant can have fleas, but a flea can't have elephants!

—— & ——

Q: Why can't an elephant ride a bicycle?

A: He doesn't have a thumb to ring the bell.

9

School Daze

Teacher: Now, what would you call a person who eats only vegetables?
Student: A vegetarian.
Teacher: And what about a man who eats people?
Student: He's a humanitarian.

— & —

Teacher: What is commonly called brain food?
Student: Noodle soup.

— & —

Teacher: Name a liquid that can't freeze.
Student: Hot water.

Teacher: Name five members of the cat family.
Student: Mother cat, father cat, and three kittens.

— & —

Teacher: I've had to punish you every day this week. What have you got to say?
Student: I'm glad it is Friday!

— & —

Teacher: How many seasons are there in a year?
Student: Two—baseball and football.

— & —

Teacher: Why are you crawling into class?
Student: Because the class has already started and you said, "Don't anyone dare walk into my class late!"

— & —

Teacher: What are the four main food groups?
Student: Canned, frozen, instant, and lite.

— & —

Teacher: This essay on your pet cat is word for word the same as your brother's.
Student: It's the same cat.

Teacher: Who can name two cities that are in Kentucky?

Student: Okay! I'll name one Dave and the other one Irving.

—— & ——

Teacher: Put your name in the upper right-hand corner of the paper and put the date in the upper left-hand corner of the paper.

Student: Boy, if he had stopped there I would have gotten a hundred on the exam.

—— & ——

Teacher: Robert Burns wrote "To a Field Mouse."

Student: I'll bet he didn't get an answer.

—— & ——

Teacher: Name me an old-time settler in the west.

Student: The sun.

—— & ——

Teacher: Now, you must not say, "I ain't goin'." You should say, "I am not going; he is not going; we are not going; they are not going."

Student: Wow! Ain't nobody goin' then?

10

What's in a Name?

What do you call a guy who bows down before the king?
Neil.

— & —

What do you call a guy who sticks his right arm into a lion's mouth?
Lefty.

— & —

What do you call a guy who likes to hike a lot?
Walker.

— & —

What do you call a guy who is very sarcastic?
Kurt.

What do you call a guy whose head is shaped like a flower?
Bud.

What do you call a guy who has been struck by lightning?
Rod.

— & —

What do you call a guy who makes diamond rings?
Jules.

— & —

What do you call a guy who votes things down all the time?
Vito.

— & —

What do you call a guy who makes loudspeakers?
Mike.

What do you call a guy who is a bullfighter?
Gord.

What do you call a guy who sat out all night on the grass?
Dewey.

What do you call a guy who is a cattle thief?
Russell.

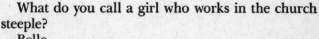

What do you call a guy who likes to see sunrises?
Don.

What do you call a girl who likes lots of butter on her bread?
Marge.

What do you call a girl who works in the church steeple?
Belle.

What do you call a girl who is in charge of the water faucet?
Flo.

What do you call a girl who complains a lot?
Mona.

— & —

What do you call a girl who likes to go sailing?
Gail.

— & —

What do you call a girl who has to be helped around a lot?
Carrie.

— & —

What do you call a girl with a big head?
Heddy.

— & —

What do you call a girl who dresses in the latest fashions?
Maude.

Hoarse Laughs

Justin: I crossed an owl with a cat.
Jake: What did you get?
Justin: An owley cat.

— & —

Q: Why do so many people have chips on their shoulders?
A: Because there's wood higher up.

— & —

Q: If you ran into a three-headed alien, what would you say?
A: Good-bye, good-bye, good-bye!

Isaac: One of my pigs was sick, so I gave him a piece of sugar.

Ingrid: Why did you do that?

Isaac: Haven't you ever heard of sugar-cured ham?

—— & ——

Q: Why did the elephant paint himself all different colors?

A: So he could hide in a package of M & M's.

—— & ——

Albert: What's the difference between an elephant and a matterbaby?

Amanda: What's a matterbaby?

Albert: Nothing, dear. What's the matter with you?

—— & ——

Wilbur: Did you hear the joke about the boy who fell on the potato-chip bag?

Wanda: No.

Wilbur: It's crumby.

—— & ——

Q: When they take your appendix out, it is an appendectomy. When they remove your tonsils from your throat, it is a tonsillectomy. What is it when you remove growth from your head?

A: A haircut

Abner: The fellow I used to work for is the politest man in the world.

Agatha: Why do you say that?

Abner: He sent me a telegram that read, "You're fired. Best regards!"

—— & ——

Q: Why do flamingos stand on one leg?

A: Because if they picked up the other leg, they would fall over!

—— & ——

Rich man: No, I will not tell you what time it is!

Young man: Well, and why not?

Rich man: Because if I tell you what time it is, you'll start a conversation. You'll ask me what my business is, and I'll tell you. Then I'll have to ask yours, even though I'm not the least bit interested. Pretty soon we'll be right chummy. I'll get off at Wilson Avenue, where I live, and you'll get off, too. My wife will be waiting for me in the car. I'll introduce you. My wife will invite you to come along to the house for tea. Then she'll invite you to stay for dinner and you'll accept. You'll meet my lovely daughter and fall in love with her. You'll probably propose and ask her to marry you. And I don't want any man to marry my daughter who doesn't own a watch.

Young Man: Oh. So, what is your business?

Q: What is the best cure for insomnia?
A: Just keep sleeping it off.

—— & ——

Kermit: Did you hear the story about Captain Billy?
Stella: No, what happened?
Kermit: When Captain Billy went to sea, his family kept a light burning in the window for 20 years.
Stella: Twenty years! That's a long time.
Kermit: Yeah. When he finally returned home, his family gave him a royal welcome and an electric bill for $9,786.

—— & ——

Neighbor boy: I've run away from home. I'm going to live with you from now on.
Neighbor: What will your parents say?
Neighbor boy: Nothing. We drew your name out of a hat.

—— & ——

Q: What did the leopard say after he finished his lunch?
A: Mm-mm-mm-mm! That just hit the right spot!

—— & ——

Derek: I don't know whether to take a job in a barbershop or to spend my time writing novels.
Dorcus: Toss a coin...heads or tales.

Jody the joker: Did you happen to see a wagon load of monkeys go by?
Jake: Nope, why, did you fall off?

— & —

Lisa: Take some friendly advice.
Bob: What's that?
Lisa: Send your wits out to be sharpened.

12

What Am I?

Q: The more you crack me, the more people like you. What am I?

A: A smile.

— & —

Q: I have six eyes, two mouths, and three ears. What am I?

A: Ugly.

— & —

Q: I've got five arms, six heads, three eyes, and two noses. What am I?

A: A liar.

Q: I am something that has three feet, and yet I am unable to walk. What am I?

A: A yardstick.

—— & ——

Q: I am something that is filled every morning and emptied every night, except once a year when I am filled at night and emptied in the morning. What am I?

A: A Christmas stocking.

—— & ——

Q: I am something everyone overlooks no matter how careful he is. What am I?

A: Your nose.

—— & ——

Q: Take away my first letter; take away my second letter; take away all my letters, and I remain the same. What am I?

A: The postman.

—— & ——

Q: I am something that comes with a train, goes with a train, is of no use to the train, and yet the train can't go without me. What am I?

A: Noise.

Q: I am something that has a head and a tail, but no body. What am I?
A: A penny.

—— & ——

Q: I am forever, and yet was never. What am I?
A: Eternity.

—— & ——

Q: I am something that is known all over the world, and I have a name of three letters. Strangely enough, when two of my letters are taken away, I still have the same name. What am I?
A: Tea.

—— & ——

Q: I am something that a girl often looks for, but always hopes she won't find. What am I?
A: A run in her stocking.

—— & ——

Q: Those who have me not, do not wish for me. Those who have me do not wish to lose me. Those who win me have me no longer. What am I?
A: A lawsuit.

13

Ken & Melba

Ken: What stays hot even if you put it in a refrigerator?
Melba: I have no clue.
Ken: A pepper.

— *&* —

Ken: What is a bee with a low buzz?
Melba: I don't know.
Ken: A mumble bee.

— *&* —

Ken: What animal has two humps and is found at the North Pole?
Melba: Beats me.
Ken: A lost camel.

Ken: What has three wings, three eyes, and two beaks?

Melba: I can't guess.

Ken: A bird with spare parts.

— & —

Ken: What room has no floors, no walls, and no windows?

Melba: I have no idea.

Ken: A mushroom.

— & —

Ken: What did the baby sardine say when he saw a submarine?

Melba: You tell me.

Ken: Look! There's a can of people!

— & —

Ken: What is the least dangerous kind of robbery?

Melba: I give up.

Ken: A safe robbery.

— & —

Ken: What do you call two people riding bikes together?

Melba: Who knows?
Ken: Cyclamates.

—— & ——

Ken: What is the hardest thing about learning to roller skate?
Melba: You've got me.
Ken: The pavement.

—— & ——

Ken: What is that thing which you cannot hold for five minutes, yet it is as light as a feather?
Melba: My mind is a blank.
Ken: Your breath.

—— & ——

Ken: What is a forum?
Melba: That's a mystery.
Ken: Two-um plus two-um.

—— & ——

Ken: What bird is the biggest coward?
Melba: I'm blank.
Ken: A canary, because it is yellow.

—— & ——

Ken: What should you carry on a long hike in the desert?

Melba: I don't have the foggiest.
Ken: A thirst-aid kit.

—— & ——

Ken: What is the difference between a cat and a comma?
Melba: It's unknown to me.
Ken: A cat has claws at the end of its paws, but a comma has a pause at the end of its clause.

—— & ——

Ken: What relaxes a chess player?
Melba: I'm in the dark.
Ken: Taking a knight off.

—— & ——

Ken: What step did the man do when he walked across a patch of wet tar?
Melba: Search me.
Ken: The goo-step!

—— & ——

Ken: What is shaped like a finger, and is the same color and size of a finger?
Melba: You've got me guessing.
Ken: A thumb.

Ken: What kind of a house weighs the least?
Melba: I pass.
Ken: A lighthouse.

—— & ——

Ken: What do you call a girl who has three boy-friends named William?
Melba: How should I know?
Ken: A Bill collector.

—— & ——

Ken: What is the difference between the sun and bread?
Melba: I don't know.
Ken: The sun rises in the east, and the bread rises with the yeast.

14

Crazy Definitions

Laplander: The most awkward man on a crowded bus.

— & —

Kindred: Fear that relatives are coming to stay.

— & —

Irish red hair: Scarlet O'Hara.

— & —

Locate: Nickname for a short girl named Catherine.

Nepotism: A form of favoritism—relatively.

— & —

Net income: The money a fisherman earns

— & —

Overeating: An activity that will make you thick to your stomach.

— & —

Paradise: Two ivory cubes with dots all over them.

— & —

Pasteurize: Too far to see.

— & —

Pillow: A nap sack.

— & —

Plagiarist: A man whose scissors are sharper than his wits.

— & —

Restitution: An institution where you can go and get a good rest.

Ringleader: First in the family to take a bath on Saturday night.

— & —

Sarcasm: Barbed ire.

— & —

Selfishness: A state of mine.

— & —

Slogan: A revolver that shoots lazy bullets.

— & —

Square meal: A TV dinner.

— & —

Steering committee: Four people trying to park a car.

— & —

T: The difference between here and there.

— & —

Chatterbox: Another name for a telephone booth.

— & —

Vegetarian: A good salad citizen.

15

Open the Door!

Knock, knock.
Who's there?
You.
You who?
You who yourself!

— & —

Knock, knock.
Who's there?
Wooden shoe.
Wooden shoe who?
Wooden shoe like to know?

— & —

Knock, knock.
Who's there.

Rufus.
Rufus who?
Rufus leaking, and I'm getting wet.

— & —

Knock, knock.
Who's there?
Alison.
Alison who?
Alison Wonderland.

— & —

Knock, knock.
Who's there?
Ivor.
Ivor who?
Ivor sore hand from knocking on this door.

— & —

Knock, knock.
Who's there?
Hair combs.
Hair combs who?
Hair combs the judge! Hair combs the judge!

— & —

Knock, knock.
Who's there?

Eddie.
Eddie who?
Eddie body home?

— & —

Knock, knock.
Who's there?
Police.
Police who?
Police open the door.

— & —

Knock, knock.
Who's there?
Domino.
Domino who?
Domino cowhand...from the Rio Grand.

— & —

Knock, knock.
Who's there?
Weirdo.
Weirdo who?
Weirdo you think you're going?

— & —

Knock, knock.
Who's there?
Justin

Justin who?
Justin time for your dinner.

— & —

Knock, knock.
Who's there?
Elsie.
Elsie who?
Elsie you around.

— & —

Knock, knock.
Who's there?
Franz.
Franz who?
Franz, Romans, countrymen...

16

Odds & Ends

Pilot trainer: Tomorrow, you will begin flying solo.
Pupil: Really? How close to the ground is that?

— & —

Valerie: Has anyone lost $50?
Vanessa: I have.
Valerie: Where did you lose it?
Vanessa: Where you found it.

— & —

Alec: I know everything there is to know about tennis.
Alma: Okay—how many holes are there in a tennis net?

Brice: My brother is such a bad driver.
Darren: How bad is he?
Brice: When he went to get his license, he got four tickets on the written test alone.

—— & ——

Q: Why was the mother owl worried about her boy?
A: Because he didn't give a hoot about anything.

—— & ——

Eli: I haven't spoken to my wife in two weeks.
Wade: How come?
Eli: I don't like to interrupt her.

—— & ——

Rookie employee: How do you make a car top?
Factory employee: You tep on the brake, tupid!

—— & ——

Q: Will February March?
A: No, but April May before June.

—— & ——

Gladys: Have you seen some of her dates?
Glenda: No, what do they look like?
Gladys: Let's put it this way, I don't know whether to shake their hands or try to teach them tricks.

Q: What is the favorite dessert of most carpenters and boxers?

A: Pound cake.

— & —

Q: How do people who go hang-gliding for the first time end up feeling?

A: Soar all over.

— & —

Q: What do you get when you cross poison ivy and a four-leaf clover?

A: A rash of good luck.

— & —

Patient: I think I have something in my eye.

Doctor: Did your mother ever have something in her eye?

Patient: Yes.

Doctor: Did your father ever have something in his eye?

Patient: Yes.

Doctor: There's your problem. It runs in the family.

17

Maynard & Myrtle

Maynard: What is a boxer's favorite drink?
Myrtle: I have no clue.
Maynard: Punch.

— *&* —

Maynard: What insect is religious?
Myrtle: I don't know.
Maynard: A praying mantis.

— *&* —

Maynard: What did the dog get when he swallowed the watch?
Myrtle: Beats me.
Maynard: He got a lot of ticks.

Maynard: What person is always hurrying?
Myrtle: I can't guess.
Maynard: A Russian.

—— & ——

Maynard: What is the difference between a prize-fighter and a man with a cold?
Myrtle: I have no idea.
Maynard: One knows his blows, and the other blows his nose.

—— & ——

Maynard: What is the end of life?
Myrtle: You tell me.
Maynard: The letter E.

—— & ——

Maynard: What is the meaning of lemonade?
Myrtle: I give up.
Maynard: When you help an old lemon cross the street.

—— & ——

Maynard: What is the best way to get to the hospital?
Myrtle: Who knows?
Maynard: Stand in the middle of traffic!

Maynard: What happened when Abel died?
Myrtle: You've got me.
Maynard: He became unable.

—— & ——

Maynard: What makes you think a man is getting taller?
Myrtle: My mind is a blank.
Maynard: His head is sticking up through his hair!

—— & ——

Maynard: What is the hardest work some people do before breakfast?
Myrtle: That's a mystery.
Maynard: Getting up.

—— & ——

Maynard: What inventions have helped people get up in the world?
Myrtle: I'm blank.
Maynard: The elevator, the ladder, and the alarm clock.

—— & ——

Maynard: What is the coldest row in the theater?
Myrtle: I don't have the foggiest.
Maynard: Z-Row (zero).

Maynard: What would you have if a bird got caught in a lawn mower?
Myrtle: It's unknown to me.
Maynard: Shredded tweet.

— & —

Maynard: What is the healthiest kind of water?
Myrtle: I'm in the dark.
Maynard: Well water.

— & —

Maynard: What did the property owner say to the trespasser?
Myrtle: Search me.
Maynard: Leave my site at once!

— & —

Maynard: What did the boy say when he decided to sell his bicycle?
Myrtle: You've got me guessing.
Maynard: I think I'll peddle my bike.

— & —

Maynard: What farm animal is a cannibal?
Myrtle: I pass.
Maynard: A cow. It eats its fodder.

Maynard: What fish is a very evil fish?
Myrtle: How should I know?
Maynard: A devilfish.

18

The Answer Man

Q: Why does your mother always buy maple furniture?
A: Because they don't make strawberry or vanilla.

— & —

Q: Why was the horse going to Hollywood?
A: He wanted to play bit parts in the movies.

— & —

Q: Why did the man buy his son a dachshund?
A: He wanted to get him a down-to-earth pet.

— & —

Q: Why did the boy wear his hat over his ears?
A: He wanted to hear the band.

Q: Why couldn't the housewife find gloves big enough to fit her?
A: Because she had dishpan hands.

—— & ——

Q: Why did the gardener throw roses into the burning building?
A: He had heard that flowers grow better in hot houses.

—— & ——

Q: Why is a healthy boy like the United States?
A: Because he has a good constitution.

—— & ——

Q: Why did the grocer sue the pelican?
A: Because the pelican had too big a bill.

—— & ——

Q: Why did the bank robber take a bath?
A: So he could make a clean getaway.

—— & ——

Q: Why did the whale cross the ocean?
A: To get to the other tide.

Q: Why did the girl sit on her watch?
A: She wanted to be on time.

— & —

Q: Why do bees have sticky hair?
A: Because they use honeycombs.

— & —

Q: Why did the chicken cross the playground?
A: To get to the other slide.

— & —

Q: Why did the workers at the government mint go on strike?
A: They wanted to make less money.

— & —

Q: Why must it be difficult to eat soup with a moustache?
A: Because it is quite a strain.

— & —

Q: Why should a fisherman always be wealthy?
A: Because all his business is net profit.

Q: Why does a calf wag its tail?
A: Because it wants to.

— & —

Q: Why do the carpenters believe there is no such thing as stone?
A: Because they never saw it.

— & —

Q: Why wasn't the girl afraid of the shark?
A: Because it was a man-eating shark.

— & —

Q: Why does a dressmaker never lose her hooks?
A: Because she has an eye for each of them.

— & —

Q: Why does a man, just shaved, look like a brute?
A: Because he has a bare (bear) face.

— & —

Q: Why are the tallest people always the laziest?
A: Because they are longer in bed than others.

— & —

Q: Why is an airline pilot like a football player?
A: They both want to make safe touchdowns.

19

Tell Me How!

Q: Did you hear about the big fight at the candy store?
A: Yeah, a lollypop got licked.

— & —

Q: How can you best learn the value of money?
A: By trying to borrow some.

— & —

Q: How can you make seven even?
A: Take away the letter S.

— & —

Q: How do you make Mexican chili?
A: Take him to the North Pole.

Q: How did the big mountain know that the little mountain was fibbing?
A: Because it was only a bluff.

— & —

Q: How long should an animal's legs be?
A: Long enough to reach the ground.

— & —

Q: How does an octopus go to war?
A: Armed.

— & —

Q: How do you make a Maltese cross?
A: Pull its tail.

— & —

Q: How did Jonah feel when the whale swallowed him?
A: Down in the mouth.

— & —

Q: How did the man feel when he received a big bill from the electric company?
A: He was shocked.

Q: How does an Irish potato change its nationality?
A: It gets French-fried.

— & —

Q: How can you make varnish disappear?
A: Take out the R.

— & —

Q: How many I's are there in Mississippi?
A: Count the people, and then multiply by two.

— & —

Q: How can you cut a telescope in half?
A: With a seesaw.

— & —

Q: How can you get a cow into a frying pan?
A: Use shortening.

— & —

Q: How can you have bread if you are on a liquid diet?
A: Drink a toast.

— & —

Q: How do you make a slow horse fast?
A: Stop feeding him.

Q: How can you keep fish from smelling?
A: Cut off their noses.

—— & ——

Q: How can a caterpillar get out of a jar when the lid is on?
A: Let it run around until it wears itself out.

—— & ——

Q: How can you go out of the room with two legs and come back with six?
A: Bring a chair back with you.

20

When, When, When?

Q: When is a man like a pony?
A: When he is a little hoarse.

— & —

Q: When a lady faints, what number will restore her?
A: You must bring her 2.

— & —

Q: When is a good time for someone to lose his temper?
A: When it becomes bad.

— & —

Q: When is an elevator not an elevator?
A: When it is going down.

Q: When is it socially correct to serve milk in a saucer?
A: When you give it to a cat.

—— & ——

Q: When is an operation funny?
A: When it leaves the patient in stitches.

—— & ——

Q: When can't astronauts land on the moon?
A: When it is full.

—— & ——

Q: When is a green book not a green book?
A: When it is read.

—— & ——

Q: When is the time of day like the whistle of a train?
A: When it is two to two.

—— & ——

Q: When did the fly fly?
A: When the spider spied her.

—— & ——

Q: When things seem wrong, what can you always count on?
A: Your fingers.

Q: When is water most likely to escape?
A: When it is only half-tide.

— & —

Q: When is a shoemaker like a doctor?
A: When he is heeling.

— & —

Q: When are the police called to the City Hall lawn?
A: When the grass begins to shoot.

— & —

Q: When do you charge a new battery?
A: When you can't pay cash.

— & —

Q: When a little boy puts his socks on wrong side out, what does his mother do?
A: She turns the hose on him.

— & —

Q: When is a wall like a fish?
A: When it is scaled.

— & —

Q: When is coffee like the soil?
A: When it is ground.

Q: When is a shellfish stronger than a shark?
A: When it's all mussel.

—— & ——

Q: When has a man the right to scold his coffee?
A: When he has more than sufficient grounds.

—— & ——

Q: When was beef the highest?
A: When the cow jumped over the moon.

—— & ——

Q: When should a boy kick about something he gets for his birthday?
A: When he gets a football.

—— & ——

Q: When is a baseball catcher like a farmer?
A: When he chases a foul.

—— & ——

Q: When is longhand quicker than shorthand?
A: When it's on a clock.

—— & ——

Q: When is a farmer cruel to his corn?
A: At harvest time, when he must pull its ears.

21

Christy & Lisa

Christy: What runs around town all day and lies down all night with its tongue hanging out?
Lisa: I have no clue.
Christy: Your shoe.

— & —

Christy: What does a farmer grow if he works hard?
Lisa: I don't know.
Christy: Tired.

— & —

Christy: What do you call the person who mows the grass of a baseball field?
Lisa: Beats me.
Christy: A diamond cutter.

Christy: What musical instrument invites you to fish?
Lisa: I can't guess.
Christy: Cast-a-net.

— & —

Christy: What binds two people together, yet only touches one?
Lisa: I have no idea.
Christy: A wedding ring.

— & —

Christy: What is the difference between a book and a talkative bore?
Lisa: You tell me.
Christy: You can shut up the book.

— & —

Christy: What did the eye say to the ice cube?
Lisa: I give up.
Christy: Icy you!

— & —

Christy: What did the train engine say when it had a cold?
Lisa: Who knows?
Christy: A-choo, a-choo, a-choo-choo-choo.

Christy: What is the quietest game in the world?
Lisa: You've got me.
Christy: Bowling. You can hear a pin drop.

— & —

Christy: What state always seems to be in poor health?
Lisa: My mind is a blank.
Christy: Ill.

— & —

Christy: What is a ticklish subject?
Lisa: That's a mystery.
Christy: The study of feathers.

— & —

Christy: What do Indians raise that you can get lost in?
Lisa: I'm blank.
Christy: Maize (maze).

— & —

Christy: What animal talks a lot?
Lisa: I don't have the foggiest.
Christy: A yackety yak.

Christy: What did the termite say when he saw a house burning?

Lisa: It's unknown to me.

Christy: Barbecue tonight!

— & —

Christy: What do snakes do after they have a fight?

Lisa: I'm in the dark.

Christy: They hiss and make up.

— & —

Christy: What falls all day yet never gets hurt?

Lisa: Search me.

Christy: A waterfall.

— & —

Christy: What do you call a person who thinks he has wings and can fly?

Lisa: You've got me guessing.

Christy: Plane crazy.

— & —

Christy: What kind of motorcycle do comedians ride?

Lisa: I pass.

Christy: A Yamaha-ha-ha.

Christy: What's the funniest animal in the world?
Lisa: How should I know?
Christy: A stand-up chameleon.

—— & ——

Christy: What country is popular on Thanksgiving Day?
Lisa: I don't know.
Christy: Turkey.

22

Belly Laughs

Little brother: Mom, did you say that my little sister has your eyes and daddy's nose?
Mother: Yes, dear, why?
Little brother: Well, now she has grandfather's teeth!

—— & ——

A celebrity is a person who works all his life to become famous enough to be recognized. Then he goes around in dark glasses so no one will know who he is.

—— & ——

Q: How do you keep a dog from barking in the back of the car?
A: Put him in the front seat.

Q: If a head of cabbage, a tomato, and a faucet ran a race, who would win?

A: The cabbage would be ahead, the tomato would ketchup, and the faucet would still be running.

— & —

Boy: Mister, can I have some boirdseed?

Clerk: Come back when you can learn to say it right.

Boy (next day): Mister, can I have some boirdseed?

Clerk: That's still not right. Come back tomorrow when you can say it right.

Boy (next day): Mister, can I have some boirdseed?

Clerk: No. No. I won't sell you any birdseed until you can say it right. Come back tomorrow.

Boy (next day): Mister, would you like to buy a dead boird?

— & —

Officer at the shooting range: Get ready. Aim. Fire at will.

Soldier: Which one is Will?

— & —

Officer: Does your uniform fit you satisfactorily?

Soldier: The shirt is all right, sir, but the pants are a little tight around the armpits.

— & —

David: Would you rather be in an explosion or a collision?

Zack: A collision. In a collision—there you are, but in an explosion—where are you?

— & —

Amy: I'm sure glad I wasn't born in Germany.
Peggy: Why is that?
Amy: Because I don't speak German.

— & —

Cindy: I had the radio on last night.
Larry: Really? How did it fit?

— & —

Customer: How much is that duck?
Salesman: He costs $20.
Customer: I'll take it. Will you send me the bill?
Salesman: No way! You'll have to buy the whole duck!

— & —

Steve: I call my girl "Peach."
Paul: Why? Because she is so sweet?
Steve: No. She has a heart of stone.

— & —

Herbert: Check out this great camera I bought. I've already taken 300 pictures this week.

Jerome: I bet it cost a lot of money to develop all that film.
Herbert: Film?

—— & ——

Q: Mr. Alfonse is a butcher. He is 5 feet, 11 inches tall. He wears a size-12 shoe. What does he weigh?
A: He weighs meat.

—— & ——

Boy: Dad, is it true that the law of gravity keeps us on the earth?
Father: Yes. That is true.
Boy: What did we do before the law was passed?

—— & ——

First cannibal: I don't care for your friend.
Second cannibal: That's okay, just eat the vegetables!

—— & ——

Hickory, dickory, dock,
Three mice ran up the clock.
The clock struck one ... they called 911,
And the other two escaped with minor injuries.

23

Mork & Dork

Mork: What is the difference between an auction sale and seasickness?
Dork: I have no clue.
Mork: One is a sale of effects, and the other, the effects of a sail.

— & —

Mork: What fish is a heavenly fish?
Dork: Beats me.
Mork: An angelfish.

— & —

Mork: What is blue and white and has red dots?
Dork: I can't guess.
Mork: Uncle Sam with the measles.

Mork: What does a worm do in the cornfield?
Dork: I have no idea.
Mork: It goes in one ear and out the other.

— & —

Mork: What kind of pigeon sits a lot?
Dork: You tell me.
Mork: A stool pigeon.

— & —

Mork: What is bright green and has two legs and a trunk?
Dork: I give up.
Mork A seasick tourist.

— & —

Mork: What fish can pelicans eat?
Dork: Who knows?
Mork: Anything that fits the bill.

— & —

Mork: What did the big firecracker say to the little firecracker?
Dork: You've got me.
Mork: My pop is bigger than your pop.

Mork: What nail doesn't a carpenter like to hit?
Dork: My mind is a blank.
Mork: His fingernail.

— & —

Mork: Where do frogs sit?
Dork: That's a mystery.
Mork: On toadstools.

— & —

Mork: What do you want to take your cod liver oil with this morning?
Dork: I'm blank.
Mork: A spoon.

— & —

Mork: What kind of bath do you take without water?
Dork: I don't have the foggiest.
Mork: A sun bath.

— & —

Mork: What kind of dog goes to the bowling alley?
Dork: It's unknown to me.
Mork: A setter.

— & —

Mork: What animal gets the most use of its food?
Dork: I'm in the dark.
Mork: The giraffe. A little goes a long way.

Mork: What do people do in a clock factory?
Dork: Search me.
Mork: They make faces all day.

—— & ——

Mork: What kind of spy hangs around department stores?
Dork: You've got me guessing.
Mork: A counterspy.

—— & ——

Mork: What kind of dance does a bun do?
Dork: I pass.
Mork: Abundance.

—— & ——

Mork: What is a dance for two containers?
Dork: How should I know?
Mork: The can-can.

—— & ——

Mork: The more there is of it, the less you see it. What is it?
Dork: I don't know.
Mork: Darkness.

24

Use the Doorbell!

Knock, knock.
Who's there?
Theodore.
Theodore who?
Theodore is closed, open up!

—— & ——

Knock, knock.
Who's there?
Lemon juice.
Lemon juice who?
Lemon juice you to my friend!

—— & ——

Knock, knock.
Who's there?

Turnip.
Turnip who?
Turnip the heat, it's cold in here!

— & —

Knock, knock.
Who's there?
Dishwasher.
Dishwasher who?
Dishwashn't the way I shpoke before I had falsh teeth.

— & —

Knock, knock.
Who's there?
Sacha.
Sacha who?
Sacha fuss, just because I knocked at your door.

— & —

Knock, knock.
Who's there?
Butcher.
Butcher who?
Butcher arms around me, honey, and hold me tight.

— & —

Knock, knock.
Who's there?
Noah.

Noah who?
Noah good place we can go for dinner?

— & —

Knock, knock.
Who's there?
Izzy.
Izzy who?
Izzy come, izzy go.

— & —

Knock, knock.
Who's there?
Howie.
Howie who?
I'm fine, how are you?

— & —

Knock, knock.
Who's there?
Tick.
Tick who?
Tick um up. I'm a tongue-tied cowboy.

— & —

Knock, knock.
Who's there?
Isabel.
Isabel who?
Isabel ringing?

Knock, knock.
Who's there?
Diesel.
Diesel who?
Diesel all make you laugh if you aren't very bright!

—— & ——

Knock, knock.
Who's there?
Phillip.
Phillip who?
Phillip the tank—I'm out of gas!

25

Foolishness

Morris: Did you get any interesting cards this year?
Louise: Yes, we received a card from the savings-and-loan bank where we have our mortgage. It read, "Merry Christmas from our house to our house."

—— & ——

Clay: I had a buddy who had relatives in Australia. They sent him a boomerang.
Stewart: Ooh, that's neat.
Clay: He didn't like it, but every time he tried to throw it away, he hurt himself.

—— & ——

A lady tourist: I've been admiring your necklace. Do you mind me asking what it is made of?
Indian: Alligator teeth.

A lady tourist: Oh, my. Well, I suppose they hold the same meaning for you as pearls do for us.

Indian: Not quite. Anybody can open an oyster.

—— & ——

Q: How do two kangaroos live?
A: Hoppily ever after.

—— & ——

Q: What do you think the bone of contention is in most arguments?
A: The one between the ears.

—— & ——

Caroline: I'm going to give you a piece of my mind!
Ralph: Darling, do you think you can spare it?

—— & ——

Did you hear about the mother lion who asked her son Junior what he was chasing. He told her he was chasing a hunter around the tree. His mother became furious. "Haven't I told you not to play with your food?"

—— & ——

Ricky: I snore so loud I wake myself up every night.
Jimmy: Try sleeping in another room.

Trent: Did you change the water in the goldfish bowl?

Brent: They didn't drink it all yet.

—— & ——

Beverly: Did you like the second act of the play?

Christy: I didn't see it. The program said, "Second Act—Two years later," so I left.

—— & ——

Q: What do you think children feel is a well-balanced meal?

A: A hamburger in each hand.

—— & ——

King: You have offended me, and I condemn you to death.

Fool: Death!

King: Okay, you have been a good fool, so I will let you choose the manner of your death.

Fool: I choose to die of old age.

—— & ——

Patient: Oh, doctor, I have terrible troubles. I do hope that you can help me.

Psychiatrist: Now calm down. Just lie down on the couch and tell me all about your troubles.

Patient: Well, doctor, I have a duplex penthouse

apartment on Park Avenue and a summer house on the beach at Westhampton. I drive a Rolls-Royce, and my wife has a Jaguar. My two daughters go to the finest private school in the city. We belong to three very swanky clubs, and every year I manage to spend a month in Europe.

Psychiatrist: These things are very wonderful, but let's get down to your basic trouble.

Patient: I was just getting to it, doctor. You see, I only make $75 a week!

—— & ——

Q: There is a donkey on one side of a deep river, and a bundle of hay on the other side. How can the donkey get the hay? There is no bridge, and he cannot swim. Do you give up?

A: So did the other donkey.

—— & ——

Mr. Ortman: The Chinese make it an invariable rule to settle all their debts on New Year's Day.

Mr. Anderson: So I understand, but then the Chinese don't have Christmas the week before.

—— & ——

Q: It has a head like a cat, feet like a cat, a tail like a cat, but it isn't a cat. What is it?

A: A kitten.

Carlson: I have in my hand two U.S. coins which total 55 cents. One is not a nickel. What are the two coins?

Yancey: I don't know.

Carlson: One is a 50-cent piece—the other is a nickel.

26

Mark & Ryan

Mark: What is the poorest kind of plant?
Ryan: I have no clue.
Mark: A vine, because it can't support itself.

—— & ——

Mark: What kinds of stockings do baseball players like to wear?
Ryan: I don't know.
Mark: Stockings with runs in them.

—— & ——

Mark: What did the dirt say to the rain?
Ryan: Beats me.
Mark: If you keep this up, my name will be mud!

Mark: What do you call a jacket that goes up in flames?
Ryan: I can't guess.
Mark: A blazer.

—— & ——

Mark: What do you get if you cross a parrot with a canary?
Ryan: I have no idea.
Mark: A bird that knows both the words and the music.

—— & ——

Mark: What did the horse say when he got to the bottom of his nose bag?
Ryan: You tell me.
Mark: That's the last straw!

—— & ——

Mark: What do people sing in their bathtubs?
Ryan: I give up.
Mark: Soap operas.

—— & ——

Mark: What state is round at both ends and high in the middle?
Ryan: Who knows?
Mark: Ohio.

Mark: What did the electric robot say to his mother?
Ryan: You've got me.
Mark: I love you watts and watts.

— & —

Mark: What did the impatient stag say to his daughter?
Ryan: My mind is a blank.
Mark: Hurry up, deer.

— & —

Mark: What is the best way to carve wood?
Ryan: That's a mystery.
Mark: Whittle by whittle.

— & —

Mark: What goes tick tock woof, tick tock woof?
Ryan: I'm blank.
Mark: A watch dog.

— & —

Mark: What means of transportation gives people colds?
Ryan: I don't have the foggiest.
Mark: A choo-choo train.

Mark: What cake is as hard as rock?
Ryan: It's unknown to me.
Mark: Marble cake.

— & —

Mark: What is the first thing ghosts do when they get into a car?
Ryan: I'm in the dark.
Mark: They fasten their sheet belts.

— & —

Mark: What is yellow, soft, and goes round and round?
Ryan: Search me.
Mark: A long-playing omelette.

— & —

Mark: What can be held without ever being touched?
Ryan: You've got me guessing.
Mark: A conversation.

— & —

Mark: What do you call a bee born in May?
Ryan: I pass.
Mark: A maybe.

Mark: What do you call an artist who is always grumbling?
Ryan: How should I know?
Mark: Mona Lisa.

—— & ——

Mark: What do you call someone when he has got his head stuck in a bucket?
Ryan: I don't know.
Mark: Pail face.

27

The Answer Man

Q: How are a hobo and a balloon alike?
A: Both are without any visible means of support.

— & —

Q: Why is tennis such a noisy game?
A: Because each player raises a racket.

— & —

Q: Why did Santa Claus use only seven reindeer this year?
A: He left Comet home to clean the sink.

— & —

Q: Why should you be careful about telling secrets in the country?

A: Because the corn has ears, the potatoes have eyes, and the beans talk (beanstalk).

— & —

Q: Why should you expect a fisherman to be more honest than a shepherd?
A: Because a fisherman lives by hook and a shepherd lives by crook.

— & —

Q: Why is a river rich?
A: Because it has two banks.

— & —

Q: Why doesn't a steam locomotive like to sit down?
A: Because it has a tender behind.

— & —

Q: Why is being fat not funny?
A: Because you can't laugh it off.

— & —

Q: Why are identical twins like a broken alarm clock?
A: Because they are dead ringers.

— & —

Q: Why is the letter B hot?
A: Because it makes oil boil.

Q: Why does Batman brush with toothpaste?
A: To prevent bat breath.

—— & ——

Q: Why did the man put his radio in the refrigerator?
A: So he could hear cool music.

—— & ——

Q: Why do your eyes look different after being to the eye doctor?
A: Because they have been checked.

—— & ——

Q: Why was the cowboy a lot of laughs?
A: He was always horsing around.

—— & ——

Q: Why did the man put his car in the oven?
A: Because he wanted a hot rod.

—— & ——

Q: Why is the letter A like a flower?
A: Because a bee comes after it.

Q: Why did the traveler leave his watch at home when he took an airplane trip?
A: Because time flies away.

—— & ——

Q: Why did the city rat gnaw a hole in the carpet?
A: He wanted to see the floor show.

—— & ——

Q: Why is a person who never makes a wager as bad as a regular gambler?
A: Because he is no better.

—— & ——

Q: Why couldn't King Arthur find his page?
A: He had closed his book.

—— & ——

Q: Why doesn't Sweden send to other countries for cattle?
A: Because it keeps a good Stockholm.

—— & ——

Q: Why do squirrels climb trees?
A: To get away from the nuts on the ground.

28

Did You Hear About?

Stew: Did you hear about the man who walked all day and only moved two feet?

Lou: No, I didn't.

Stew: That was all he had.

— & —

Stew: Did you hear about the boy who drowned in bed?

Lou: How do you drown in bed?

Stew: Well, the bed spread, the pillow slipped, and he fell into the spring.

— & —

Stew: Did you hear about the thief who stole a calendar?

Lou: What happened to him?

Stew: He got 12 months.

Stew: Did you hear about the old lady who told knitting jokes?
Lou: No, I haven't.
Stew: She was a real nitwit.

— & —

Stew: Did you hear about the cross-eyed teacher they fired last week?
Lou: No, tell me.
Stew: She couldn't control her pupils.

— & —

Stew: Did you know it takes three sheep to make one sweater?
Lou: I didn't even know they could knit.

— & —

Stew: Did you hear the story about the man who changed his address after 40 years?
Lou: What about it?
Stew: It was a moving tale.

— & —

Stew: Did you hear about the horse who ate an electric wire instead of hay?
Lou: That's shocking!
Stew: He went haywire.

Stew: Did you hear about the angel who lost his job?
Lou: What happened to him?
Stew: He had harp failure.

—— & ——

Stew: Did you hear about the absentminded professor?
Lou: What did he do?
Stew: He returned from lunch and saw a sign on the door, "Back in 30 minutes," so he sat down and waited for himself.

29

Crazy Thoughts

Jacob: Did you hear about the man who got arrested for stealing a pig?
Lacey: How did they catch him?
Jacob: The pig squealed.

— & —

Dee Dee: Have you ever had any hobbies?
Emily: Let's see. I've had rheumatism, hives, and mumps, but I can't remember ever having hobbies.

— & —

Q: What do you call a man who laughs at his boss's jokes?
A: A man who might not have a sense of humor, but sure has a sense of direction.

Codey: I'm aching from arthritis.
Kara: How do you do? I'm Kara from Hume Lake, California.

—— & ——

Leo: Have you seen the new warning devices people are putting on their sports cars?
Lila: No, tell me about them.
Leo: The warnings read, "The keys are on the seat next to the Doberman."

—— & ——

Edgar: Did you know that rabbit is a favorite dish in Paris?
Edith: I had no idea.
Edgar: They raise them in the hutch back of Notre Dame.

—— & ——

Did you hear about the neighbor who was so grouchy her dog put up a sign that said, "Beware of Owner."

—— & ——

Q: Have you ever wondered how trains hear?
A: Through their engineers, naturally.

Customer: Do you have bacon and eggs on your menu?
Waiter: No, sir, we clean our menus every day.

— & —

Q: What would a novice bird-watcher exclaim if he spotted a large flock of geese heading south for the winter?
A: Migratious!

— & —

Christina: What do you think the toughest part of a diet is?
Christy: It sure isn't watching what you eat—it's watching what other people eat.

— & —

Mother: Willie, I wish you would run across the street and see how old Mrs. Brown is this morning.
Son: Yes'm. (Soon returning.) Mom, Mrs. Brown says it's none of your business how old she is.

— & —

Blanche: I would love for you to teach me a foreign language.
Professor: Certainly, Blanche. French, German, Russian, Italian, Spanish—
Blanche: Oh, which is the most foreign?

Son: Are caterpillars good to eat?

Father: No. What makes you ask a question like that while we are eating?

Son: You had one on your lettuce, but it's gone now.

—— & ——

Sunday school teacher: Doesn't anyone know who Peter was?

Little boy: Wasn't he a wabbit?

—— & ——

Alvin: Did you hear about the man who ran over himself?

Agnus: No, what happened?

Alvin: Well, he was standing on the corner waiting for the bus, and he asked a little boy to go across the street and buy a package of gum for him. The little boy wouldn't go, so the man ran over himself.

30

Buford & Evelyn

Buford: What dance does a hippie hate?
Evelyn: I have no clue.
Buford: A square dance.

— *&* —

Buford: What color is rain?
Evelyn: I don't know.
Buford: Water color.

— *&* —

Buford: What is green and can jump a mile in a minute?
Evelyn: Beats me.
Buford: A grasshopper with hiccups.

Buford: What did Benjamin Franklin say when he discovered electricity?
Evelyn: I can't guess.
Buford: I'm deeply shocked!

— & —

Buford: What letter is an insect?
Evelyn: I have no idea.
Buford: B.

— & —

Buford: What country mourns?
Evelyn: You tell me.
Buford: Wales.

— & —

Buford: What girl is always making blunders?
Evelyn: I give up.
Buford: Miss Take (mistake).

— & —

Buford: What is the difference between a jug of water and a man throwing his wife into the river?
Evelyn: Who knows?
Buford: One is water in the pitcher, and the other is pitch her in the water.

Buford: What animal is tiresomely talkative?
Evelyn: You've got me.
Buford: A boar.

—— & ——

Buford: What two birds are foolish?
Evelyn: My mind is a blank.
Buford: Loons and cuckoos.

—— & ——

Buford: What is the happiest state?
Evelyn: That's a mystery.
Buford: Merryland (Maryland).

—— & ——

Buford: What should we give people who are too breezy?
Evelyn: I'm blank.
Buford: The air.

—— & ——

Buford: What would you have if a goat fell into a blender?
Evelyn: I don't have the foggiest.
Buford: A mixed-up kid.

Buford: What always works with something in its eye?

Evelyn: It's unknown to me.

Buford: A needle.

— & —

Buford: What happens to a girl who doesn't know cold cream from putty?

Evelyn: I'm in the dark.

Buford: All her windows fall out.

— & —

Buford: What would happen if you swallowed uranium?

Evelyn: Search me.

Buford: You would get atomic ache (a stomach ache).

— & —

Buford: What would happen if everyone in the country bought a pink car?

Evelyn: You've got me guessing.

Buford: We would have a pink carnation.

— & —

Buford: What is the biggest jewel in the world?

Evelyn: I pass.

Buford: A baseball diamond.

Buford: What animals failed to come to Noah's Ark in pairs?
Evelyn: How should I know?
Buford: Worms. They came in apples.

—— & ——

Buford: What do you call a knife that cuts four loaves of bread at a time?
Evelyn: I don't know.
Buford: A four-loaf cleaver.

31

Where, Oh Where?

Q: Where are the kings of England usually crowned?
A: On the head.

— & —

Q: Where are the Alps?
A: Ask your mother. She puts everything away.

— & —

Q: Where would you find flying rabbits?
A: In the hare force.

— & —

Q: Where do you leave your dog when you go shopping?
A: In a barking lot.

Q: Where is a sneeze usually pointed?
A: Achoo (at you)!

—— & ——

Q: Where does a hog keep its money?
A: In piggy banks.

—— & ——

Q: Where does a fish keep its money?
A: In river banks.

—— & ——

Q: Where does an Eskimo keep his money?
A: In snowbanks.

—— & ——

Q: Where do fish wash their hands?
A: In the river basin.

—— & ——

Q: Where do chickens dance?
A: At the fowl ball.

—— & ——

Q: Where does the butcher dance?
A: At the meatball.

Q: Where do mummies go when in Arizona?
A: The Petrified Forest.

— & —

Q: Where does imitation leather come from?
A: From imitation cows.

— & —

Q: Where does all the pepper go?
A: No one nose.

— & —

Q: Where do cars get the most flat tires?
A: Where there is a fork in the road.

32

Special People

What do you call a girl who gambles all the time?
Bette.

— & —

What do you call a girl who is very conceited?
Mimi.

— & —

What do you call a girl who fell off the top of a mountain?
Dot.

— & —

What do you call a girl who likes to go to the beach?
Sandi.

What do you call a girl who likes to eat all the time?
Dinah.

— & —

What do you call a girl who likes to push around a little cart?
Dolly.

— & —

What do you call a girl who is always taking people to court?
Sue.

— & —

What do you call a girl who likes to play hide-and-go-seek?
Heidi.

— & —

What do you call a guy who makes jokes all the time?
Josh.

— & —

What do you call a guy who pretends to be blind and needs money?
Con.

What do you call a guy who does well in the stock market?
Rich.

What do you call a guy who likes to ring door bells?
Buzz.

What do you call a guy who grows vegetables?
Herb.

What do you call a guy who honks his car horn all the time?
Blair.

What do you call a guy who breaks into houses?
Jimmy.

What do you call a guy who has a bullet-proof skull?
Helmut.

What do you call a guy who works at the police station at the front desk?
Booker.

— & —

What do you call a guy who breaks dishes?
Chip.

— & —

What do you call a guy who cleans fireplaces for a living?
Cole.

— & —

What do you call a guy who is not crazy?
Norm.

— & —

What do you call a guy who likes to read books?
Red.

33

Winifred & Thaddaeus

Winifred: What pop group kills germs?
Thaddaeus: I have no clue.
Winifred: The Bleach Boys.

— *&* —

Winifred: What do you get if you cross a giant and a skunk?
Thaddaeus: I don't know.
Winifred: A big stink.

— *&* —

Winifred: What is it that is always coming but never arrives?
Thaddaeus: Beats me.
Winifred: Tomorrow. When it arrives, it is today.

Winifred: What is the difference between photographers and the whooping cough?

Thaddaeus: I can't guess.

Winifred: One makes facsimiles and the other makes sick families.

—— & ——

Winifred: What country is good for skaters?

Thaddaeus: I have no idea.

Winifred: Iceland.

—— & ——

Winifred: What country does the cook use while making dinner?

Thaddaeus: You tell me.

Winifred: Greece.

—— & ——

Winifred: What is it that is always behind time?

Thaddaeus: I give up.

Winifred: The back of a watch.

—— & ——

Winifred: What difference is there between a gardener, a billiard player, a precise man, and a church janitor?

Thaddaeus: Who knows?

Winifred: The gardener minds his peas; the billiard player, his cues; the precise man, his p's and q's; and the church janitor his keys and pews.

—— & ——

Winifred: What is the difference between a fisherman and a lazy schoolboy?

Thaddaeus: You've got me.

Winifred: One baits his hook, while the other hates his book.

—— & ——

Winifred: What do you call a donkey who carries a man?

Thaddaeus: My mind is a blank.

Winifred: A he-hauler.

—— & ——

Winifred: What ten-letter word starts with gas?

Thaddaeus: That's a mystery.

Winifred: Automobile.

—— & ——

Winifred: What did one potato chip say to the other potato chip?

Thaddaeus: I'm blank.

Winifred: Let's go for a dip!

Winifred: What was the greatest comeback in history?
Thaddaeus: I don't have the foggiest.
Winifred: Napoleon's retreat from Moscow.

— & —

Winifred: What is green and very dangerous?
Thaddaeus: It's unknown to me.
Winifred: A frog with a hand-grenade.

— & —

Winifred: What coat is put on only when it is wet?
Thaddaeus: I'm in the dark.
Winifred: A coat of paint.

— & —

Winifred: What American has had the largest family?
Thaddaeus: Search me.
Winifred: George Washington, who was the "father of his country."

— & —

Winifred: What's red and eats rocks?
Thaddaeus: I pass.
Winifred: A big red rock eater.

Winifred: What is the largest room in the world?
Thaddaeus: How should I know?
Winifred: Room for improvement.

—— & ——

Winifred: What is a hot time?
Thaddaeus: I don't know.
Winifred: A clock in an oven.

34

The
Wise Old Owl

Fox: Who was Snow White's brother?
Owl: Egg White—get the yolk?

— & —

Fox: Who is Richard Stands?
Owl: I don't know, but he must be pretty important because each morning in school we say, "I pledge allegiance to the Republic of Richard Stands."

— & —

Fox: Who has eight guns and terrorizes the ocean?
Owl: Billy the Squid.

— & —

Fox: Who is the thirstiest person in the world?
Owl: The one who drinks Canada dry.

Fox: Who lives in Australia?
Owl: Sydney.

— & —

Fox: Who is Count Dracula's favorite person on a baseball team?
Owl: The bat boy.

— & —

Fox: Who are the three unluckiest girls in the world?
Owl: Mis-chance, Mis-fortune, and Mis-hap.

— & —

Fox: Who invented the first airplane that didn't fly?
Owl: The Wrong Brothers.

35

Rib Ticklers

Cindy: Did you hear about the man who was actually cured in the doctor's waiting room?

Clyde: You're kidding, how?

Cindy: He went there with a case of amnesia and stayed in the waiting room so long, he forgot he had it.

—— & ——

Rich man: What's going on? I thought I told you to paint the porch white!

Handyman: I did paint it white. Now, how about bright red for your other car?

—— & ——

Did you hear about the movie director who made so many movies that were turkeys, they gave him an honorary Pilgrim award.

Jeremy: Your overalls are all wet.
Jerome: I know, I just washed them.
Jeremy: Then why are you wearing them?
Jerome: Because the label says: Wash and wear.

—— & ——

Emma: I'm sure glad I wasn't born in France.
Gus: Why?
Emma: Because I don't speak French.

—— & ——

Lucile: How is your little brother?
Herman: Sick in bed. He hurt himself.
Lucile: That's too bad. How did he do it?
Herman: We were playing who could lean farthest
out the window and he won.

—— & ——

Arlene: You're a sap.
Carl: What?
Arlene: You're a sap-sap-sap! You know, what
comes out of trees.
Carl: Monkeys like you.

—— & ——

Did you hear about the man named Day who mar-
ried a woman named Knight and had three children?
The oldest he called Dawn, because it was the first of

Day; the second, Moon, because it was a reflection of Day at Knight; the third, Twilight, because it was the last of Day.

— & —

Dawn: My mother is so neat.
Melody: What makes her so neat?
Dawn: If I get up to go to the bathroom in the middle of the night, when I come back my bed is made.

— & —

Duane: Honey, I know this is your first Christmas dinner, but why is it taking so long?
Ruby: Well, the cookbook said to put the turkey in the oven and turn for three hours. By the end of the first hour I was so dizzy I couldn't even *see* the oven.

— & —

There are certain kids who are the worst dressers in the world. Their favorite color is mildew.

— & —

Oscar: Boy, did you hear about the tough teacher I have?
Bert: Yeah, what about her?
Oscar: She has a black belt in teaching.

Adrian: I thought it would be so much fun to bring my boyfriend with me to a picnic that my work was sponsoring. Boy, was I wrong!

Tiffany: Gosh, what happened?

Adrian: His eating habits were so bad that even the ants stayed away.

—— & ——

Q: What is the meaning of the word unaware?

A: Unaware is what you put on first and take off last.

—— & ——

Cora: Can you lend me $10 till payday?

Cathy: I'm not sure. When is payday?

Cora: How should I know? You're the one with the job!

—— & ——

Adam: I have a hair-raising story.

Brent: Tell it to some bald-headed man then.

—— & ——

Q: What do five square meals make?

A: Round people.

—— & ——

Fay: I never have any time to myself.

Saundra: I've got five kids, and I can be alone whenever I want.

Fay: How do you manage that?
Saundra: I just start doing the dishes.

— & —

Oliver: I can lie in bed in the morning and watch the sunrise.
Chester: That's nothing. I can sit in the living room and see the kitchen sink.

— & —

Have you ever been to a restaurant where the soup is so greasy you can either eat it there or take it with you and put it in the crankcase of your car?

36

Jesse & Bessie

Jesse: What did the skunk say when the wind changed?
Bessie: I have no clue.
Jesse: It all comes back to me now.

—— *&* ——

Jesse: What should you do with a blue monster?
Bessie: I don't know.
Jesse: Cheer him up.

—— *&* ——

Jesse: What bow can never be tied?
Bessie: Beats me.
Jesse: A rainbow.

Jesse: What fish is used by a fencer?
Bessie: I can't guess.
Jesse: Swordfish.

— & —

Jesse: What is a tongue twister?
Bessie: I have no idea.
Jesse: When your tang gets all tongueled up.

— & —

Jesse: What is an astronaut's favorite meal?
Bessie: You tell me.
Jesse: Launch.

— & —

Jesse: What birds make the most noise?
Bessie: I give up.
Jesse: Whooping cranes.

— & —

Jesse: What happens to grapes that worry too much?
Bessie: Who knows?
Jesse: They get wrinkles and turn into raisins.

— & —

Jesse: What three letters in the alphabet frighten criminals?

Bessie: You've got me.
Jesse: F.B.I.

—— & ——

Jesse: What rises and waves all day?
Bessie: My mind is a blank.
Jesse: A flag.

—— & ——

Jesse: What overpowers you without hurting?
Bessie: That's a mystery.
Jesse: Sleep.

—— & ——

Jesse: What do baby apes sleep in?
Bessie: I'm blank.
Jesse: Apricots.

—— & ——

Jesse: What goes all through the house but never touches a thing?
Bessie: I don't have the foggiest.
Jesse: A voice.

—— & ——

Jesse: What do cannibals play at parties?
Bessie: It's unknown to me.
Jesse: Swallow the leader.

Jesse: What do you get if you cross a pickle and a dollar bill?

Bessie: I'm in the dark.

Jesse: Sourdough.

— & —

Jesse: What is a fast tricycle?

Bessie: Search me.

Jesse: A tot rod.

— & —

Jesse: What do you get if you cross a woodpecker and a homing pigeon?

Bessie: You've got me guessing.

Jesse: A bird that knocks on the door and delivers the message.

— & —

Jesse: What is an Italian referee?

Bessie: I pass.

Jesse: A Roman umpire.

— & —

Jesse: What do you get when you cross a lion and a parrot?

Bessie: How should I know?

Jesse: I don't know, either, but if it wants a cracker, you'd better give it one.

37

What If?

Q: If a pencil and a piece of paper had a race, which would win?

A: The pencil, because the paper would always remain stationary (stationery).

— & —

Q: If an egg came floating down the Hudson River, where did it come from?

A: From a hen.

— & —

Q: If Rumpelstiltskin likes to sit on gold, who sits on silver?

A: The Lone Ranger.

Q: If there were a bank holdup, who would be the main witness?

A: The teller.

— & —

Q: If a carpenter receives 25 cents for sawing a board into two lengths, how much should he receive for sawing the board into four lengths?

A: Seventy-five cents, because it takes only three saw cuts.

— & —

Q: If 12 make a dozen, how many make a million?

A: Very few.

— & —

Q: If you can see a duck before two ducks, a duck between two ducks, and a duck behind two ducks, how many ducks are there in all?

A: Three ducks.

— & —

Q: If you found a hundred-dollar bill in your coat pocket, what would you have?

A: Someone else's coat.

Q: If two wrongs don't make a right, what do two rights make?
A: An airplane.

— & —

Q: If you planted an angry crow, what would come up?
A: Crow-cusses.

Q: If your sister has a peach, and you have only a bite, what should you do?
A: Scratch it.

— & —

Q: If Dick's father is Bob's son, then what relation is Dick to Bob?
A: Bob is Dick's grandfather.

— & —

Q: If a hole were 17 feet wide, 15 feet long, and 35 feet deep, how much dirt would be in it?
A: None. A hole is empty.

38

Daffy Dictionary

Adam's rib: The original bone of contention.

— & —

Afternoon snack: The pause that refleshes.

— & —

Allege: A high rock shelf.

— & —

Allegro: One leg becoming longer than the other.

— & —

Antique furniture: What you get from living with children.

Atrophy: An award given to those who do not exercise.

— & —

Bathing beauty: A girl worth wading for.

— & —

Boycott: Bed for a male child.

— & —

Capsize: Same as hatsize. See also—bulkhead.

— & —

Conceit: Confidence out of control.

— & —

Conference: A meeting of the bored.

— & —

Coverage: To pretend to be older or younger than you are.

— & —

Cowardice: Yellow frozen water.

Denial: A river in Egypt.

— & —

Diet: A penalty for exceeding the feed limit.

— & —

Dogma: A mother dog.

— & —

Dollar sign: An S that has been double-crossed.

— & —

Ego trip: Stumbling over your own feet.

— & —

Family swimming pool: A small body of water completely surrounded by other people's children.

— & —

Flirtation: Wishful winking.

— & —

Forger: A man who is always ready to write a wrong.

Hari-kari: Transporting a wig from one place to another.

— *&* —

Hunger: What the posse did to the lady rustler.

— *&* —

Hypochondriac: Someone with a sick sense.

39

Ruby & Red

Ruby: What would bugs on the moon be called?
Red: I have no clue.
Ruby: Luna tics.

— & —

Ruby: What state is the cleanest?
Red: I don't know.
Ruby: Wash.

— & —

Ruby: What is the difference between a hunting dog and a locomotive?
Red: Beats me.
Ruby: One is trained to run, and the other runs a train.

Ruby: What is worse than raining cats and dogs?
Red: I can't guess.
Ruby: Hailing buses.

—— & ——

Ruby: What is it that has eight feet and can sing?
Red: I have no idea.
Ruby: A quartet.

—— & ——

Ruby: What is the difference between a professional violinist and the person who goes to hear him?
Red: You tell me.
Ruby: One plays for his pay, and the other pays for his play.

—— & ——

Ruby: What is it that passes in front of the sun yet casts no shadow?
Red: I give up.
Ruby: The wind.

—— & ——

Ruby: What is the difference between a postage stamp and a girl?
Red: Who knows?
Ruby: One is a mail fee, and the other is a female.

Ruby: What geometrical figure represents a lost parrot?

Red: You've got me.

Ruby: Polygon (polly gone).

— & —

Ruby: What is it that is very dark yet has done most to enlighten the world?

Red: My mind is a blank.

Ruby: Ink.

— & —

Ruby: What do you call a cat who drinks lemonade?

Red: That's a mystery.

Ruby: A sourpuss.

— & —

Ruby: What kind of paper will you use when you make your kite?

Red: I'm blank.

Ruby: I'd suggest flypaper.

— & —

Ruby: What's hot, has wrinkles and squares, and is very brave?

Red: I don't have the foggiest.

Ruby: Hiawaffle, the Indian.

Ruby: What is blue and dangerous?
Red: It's unknown to me.
Ruby: A bluebird with a machine gun.

— & —

Ruby: What's the best place to look for a helping hand?
Red: I'm in the dark.
Ruby: At the end of your arm.

— & —

Ruby: What is the difference between a farmer and a seamstress?
Red: Search me.
Ruby: One gathers what he sows, and the other sews what she gathers.

— & —

Ruby: What kind of doctor treats ducks?
Red: You've got me guessing.
Ruby: A quack.

— & —

Ruby: What do you call a tuba's father?
Red: I pass.
Ruby: Oom-papa.

Ruby: What do you call a man who sits on an easel?
Red: How should I know?
Ruby: Art.

— & —

Ruby: What job do hippies do?
Red: I don't know.
Ruby: They hold your leggies on.

40

Stop the Knocking!

Knock, knock.
Who's there?
Distress.
Distress who?
Distress is very short.

— & —

Knock, knock.
Who's there?
Pecan.
Pecan who?
Pecan somebody your own size.

— & —

Knock, knock.
Who's there?

Alfred.
Alfred who?
Alfred the needle if you'll sew the button on.

— & —

Knock, knock.
Who's there?
Juneau.
Juneau who?
No, I don't. Do you?

— & —

Knock, knock.
Who's there?
Kayak.
Kayak who?
You kayak if you want to.

— & —

Knock, knock.
Who's there?
Leggo.
Leggo who?
Leggo the door—I wanna come in!

— & —

Knock, knock.
Who's there?
Sue.

Sue who?
Sue Prize.

— & —

Knock, knock.
Who's there?
Duke.
Duke who?
Duke the halls with boughs of holly.

— & —

Knock, knock.
Who's there?
Major.
Major who?
Major answer the door, didn't I?

41

More Craziness

Q: Do zombies like being dead?
A: Of corpse.

— & —

Q: On what waterway did Frankenstein travel?
A: The Erie (eerie) Canal.

— & —

Q: Do fish bite at sunrise?
A: No, they bite at worms!

— & —

Q: Whose best works are trampled on?
A: A shoemaker's.

Mrs. Peacock: My car just went under some quicksand.
Insurance agent: That's all right. Don't worry about it.
Mrs. Peacock: Why not?
Insurance agent: Your car is completely covered.

—— & ——

Did you hear about the hardworking farmer and son who had saved all their lives so that the boy could go to college? After he had gone about a year, he came home for Christmas and his father wanted to know something that he had learned in college. So the boy repeated, "Pi r². " His father yelled, "Do you mean to tell me that pies are square? You know right well that pies are round. Cornbread is square."

—— & ——

Garen: I wish I could bowl as well as I play baseball.
Darren: How well can you play baseball?
Garen: Not very well. All I get are strikes!

—— & ——

Q: Why is the bathtub's nickname "Rosie"?
A: Because every time it gets used, it gets a ring around Rosie.

—— & ——

Prissy: It takes me an hour to get to work in the morning.
Merilla: Before or after you arrive?

Jordan: Camilla, I made two kinds of cookies today. Would you like to take your pick?
Camilla: No, better use a hammer.

—— & ——

Monica: Did you hear about the Chicago department store that had two Santas?
Lisa: Why did they have two Santas?
Monica: One was an express line for kids who asked for nine toys or less.

—— & ——

Q: In what month do girls talk the least?
A: February.

—— & ——

Q: Do you know how to tell a dogwood tree?
A: By his bark.

—— & ——

Little daughter: Why is father singing so much tonight?
Mother: He is trying to sing the baby to sleep.
Little daughter: Well, if I was the baby I'd pretend I was asleep.

—— & ——

Mrs. Lundgren: Reginald told me his family is a very old one. They were one of the first to come across.

Mr. Peters: The grocer told me yesterday that now they are the last to come across.

— & —

First goldfish: So I guess you're not dating that terrific-looking lobster anymore.

Second goldfish: It didn't work out. He was too shellfish.

— & —

Lacey: Grandpa, were you in the Ark?

Grandpa: Certainly not, my dear!

Lacey: Then why weren't you drowned?

— & —

Hostess: Good-bye, Gretchen. You must come again soon. We should like to see more of you.

Gretchen: But there isn't any more of me.

42

Tell Me How!

Q: How many eggs can a man eat on an empty stomach?

A: None. As soon as he begins to eat even one bite of an egg, his stomach is no longer empty.

— & —

Q: How do you make soup gold?

A: You put in 14 carrots.

— & —

Q: How do you get water into watermelons?

A: You plant them in the spring.

— & —

Q: How do you prevent an elephant from going through the eye of a needle?

A: Tie a knot in its tail.

Q: How do you get down off an elephant?
A: You don't. You get down off a duck.

— & —

Q: How do you describe pedestrians in Los Angeles?
A: Los Angeles dodgers.

— & —

Q: How does a witch tell time?
A: With a witch watch.

— & —

Q: How do fishermen make their nets?
A: They make lots of holes, and then join them together.

— & —

Q: How do you stop your feet from falling asleep?
A: Wear loud socks.

— & —

Q: How was Moses able to part the Red Sea?
A: He used a sea-saw.

— & —

Q: How do fish go into business?
A: They start on a small scale.

Q: How did Lucy get lucky?
A: She found a K.

— & —

Q: How can you tell if there is an elephant in the refrigerator?
A: The door won't shut.

— & —

Q: How did the dumb boy pass his I.Q. test?
A: He cheated.

— & —

Q: How would you describe a frog with broken legs?
A: Unhoppy.

— & —

Q: How do you get rid of a spotted dog?
A: Use a spot remover.

— & —

Q: How do you kill a blue elephant?
A: With a blue shotgun.

43

Funny Business

Terry: My little brother is only three, and he can spell his name backward already!

Barry: That's amazing. What's his name?

Terry: Otto.

— & —

Leslie: At Christmas we always exchange presents.

Julia: That's neat. It sounds like a lot of fun.

Leslie: Well, I don't know about that. I exchange the present my husband gave me, and he exchanges the one I gave him.

— & —

Q: Why were the stockings hung by the chimney with care?

A: Because he'd worn them for months, and they needed the air.

—— & ——

Cody: Hey, Kelly, did you give your mother-in-law a gift?

Kelly: Oh, yeah. I gave her an X-ray of my chest for Christmas. I just wanted to show her that my heart was in the right place.

—— & ——

Q: What do you do when the doctor tells you you're iron-deficient?

A: You take up nail-biting.

—— & ——

Dominique: Did you know that the United States can do everything any other country can?

Max: You don't say.

Dominique: Well, everything except borrow money from the United States.

—— & ——

Kenneth: Last year I explained to the children that there is no Santa Claus.

Bessie: Did they believe you?

Kenneth: Yeah, but this year I'm trying to explain it to my wife.

Did you hear about or see the ad in the *Fresno Journal*? It read: 'Twas the night before Christmas and all through the house not a creature was stirring not even a mouse. ATLAS EXTERMINATION COMPANY.

—— & ——

Customer: I want to buy a good revolver.
Owner: How about a six-shooter?
Customer: Can you make it a nine-shooter? It's for the cat next door.

—— & ——

Did you hear the story about the old farmer? He had gone to town to have dinner with his relatives. Just as he was getting ready to leave their house, a terrible blizzard struck. The snow came down so hard and fast that he couldn't see a thing.

His relatives told him that he couldn't drive in weather like that. They asked him to spend the night.

The farmer thanked them very much and was extremely relieved. He told them he would go back to the farm for his pajamas and be right back.

—— & ——

Jack: I was arrested for purse-snatching.
Hannah: You're kidding!
Jack: It was a case of mistaken identity. I didn't know she was a cop.

Page: My mom loves hand-me-downs.

Joy: Wow, so does my mom.

Page: Yeah, I was lucky to be born in my own birth-day suit.

—— & ——

Cornelius: Hand-me-downs are so embarrassing.

Henrietta: Oh come on, they're not that bad.

Cornelius: Oh yeah, I've got lint in my pockets older than I am.

—— & ——

Brandon: Did you know that they are building a new Russian restaurant on the moon?

Emily: That's great! I'm so glad!

Brandon: Don't get too excited. The food may be okay, but there won't be any atmosphere.

—— & ——

Q: What is an infant prodigy?

A: A child with highly imaginative parents.

44

The Answer Man

Q: Why did the baseball player blink his eyelashes all day?
A: He needed batting practice.

—— & ——

Q: Why did the fan bring a rope to the ball game?
A: So he could tie up the score.

—— & ——

Q: Why does a traffic signal turn red?
A: You would too if you had to change in front of all those people.

—— & ——

Q: Why did grandma put roller skates on her rocking chair?
A: Because she wanted to rock 'n' roll!

Q: Why did the letter arrive wet?
A: There was postage dew.

— & —

Q: Why should a spider make a good outfielder?
A: Because it is always catching flies.

— & —

Q: Why doesn't the ocean cover the land?
A: Because it's tied.

— & —

Q: Why is a barn so noisy?
A: Because the cows have horns.

— & —

Q: Why were the bees on strike?
A: They wanted shorter flowers and more honey.

— & —

Q: Why is Sunday the strongest day?
A: The others are weekdays.

— & —

Q: Why is a drama teacher like the Pony Express?
A: Because he is a stage coach.

Q: Why is a sinking ship like a person in jail?
A: Because it needs bailing out.

—— & ——

Q: Why was Cinderella thrown off the baseball team?
A: Because she ran away from the ball.

—— & ——

Q: Why did the chicken cross the road two times?
A: Because he was a double-crosser.

—— & ——

Q: Why did the jelly roll?
A: It saw the apple turnover.

—— & ——

Q: Why is a policeman the strongest man in the world?
A: Because he can hold up automobiles with one hand.

—— & ——

Q: Why should a doctor never be seasick?
A: Because he is so accustomed to sea (see) sickness.

Q: Why is an empty purse always the same?
A: Because there is never any change in it.

—— & ——

Q: Why don't women become bald as soon as men?
A: Because they wear their hair longer.

—— & ——

Q: Why does a giraffe have such a long neck?
A: Because his head is so far away from his body.

—— & ——

Q: What is it that can be broken without being hit or dropped?
A: A promise.

45

Silly Dillies

Deffy: My dad's always hollering what to do when I play in Little League.

Carter: Does that bother you?

Deffy: I don't stand outside his office window and yell at him how to write letters to his clients.

— & —

Zackary: Once my brother drove the wrong way on a one-way street.

Obadiah: Wow! What happened?

Zackary: I asked him if he knew where he was going. He said he did, but that he must be late...everybody else seemed to be going home.

Animal Rights Activist: Madam, do you realize some poor dumb beast suffered so that you could wear that mink coat you have on?

Madam: How dare you talk that way about my husband!

—— & ——

Lonnie: One day, my dearest, would you be my wife?

Bonnie: One day? I wouldn't be your wife for one minute of the day!

—— & ——

Maid: How do I announce dinner, ma'am? Do I say, "Dinner is ready" or "Dinner is served"?

Mistress: If it is anything like yesterday's meal, just say, "Dinner is ruined"!

—— & ——

Man to taxi driver: Can you take a joke?

Taxi driver: Of course, sir, where do you want to go?

—— & ——

Sophia: There is a girl in my class that is so skinny.

Tiffany: How skinny is she?

Sophia: She put on her fuzzy white hat and fuzzy white slippers and went out as a Q-tip.

Old lady: I want to buy a collar for my dog.
Shopkeeper: How big is your dog?
Old lady: Oh, about this big.
Shopkeeper: Why don't you bring your dog in so that we can measure him properly.
Old lady: Oh, I couldn't do that. It's going to be a surprise for him.

—— & ——

Did you hear about the two explorers who were going through the jungle when a ferocious lion jumped out in front of them?

The first explorer whispered to the second explorer to keep calm. The first explorer asked the second explorer if he remembered what they had read in the book on wild animals. "If you stand absolutely still and look the lion straight in the eye, he will turn tail and run away," said the first explorer.

The second explorer said, "Fine. You've read the book, I've read the book, but has the lion read the book?"

—— & ——

Jason: Did you ever take chloroform?
Gwen: No, who teaches it?

—— & ——

Passenger: I'd like a round-trip ticket.
Ticket agent: Where to?
Passenger: Back here, of course!

Calvin: What lovely eyes you have!

Hannah: I'm glad you like them. They were a birthday present.

—— & ——

Did you hear about the pet shop in Fresno, California that has a sign in one of its windows: "Situation Wanted: Healthy kitten wants good home—honest, loyal, sober, will do light mousework."

—— & ——

Elmer: First I got tonsillitis, followed by appendicitis and pneumonia. After that I got erysipelas with hemachromatosis. Following that I got poliomyelitis and finally ended up with neuritis. Then they gave me hypodermics and inoculations.

Erwin: Boy, you had a time!

Elmer: I'll say! I thought I'd never pull through that spelling test.

—— & ——

Chad: I'm home, Hazel. You can serve the salad.

Hazel: How did you know we were having salad?

Chad: There's no smell of burning.

—— & ——

Gabriel: I have this girl in my class who is very neat.

Geraldine: What do you mean by neat?

Gabriel: She brought a note from her mother once that asked the teacher to forgive her for being absent from school the day before. Her dress had a wrinkle.

46

Bartholomew & Reginald

Bartholomew: What animal would be likely to eat a relative?
Reginald: I have no clue.
Bartholomew: Could it be an anteater?

— & —

Bartholomew: What bird is always in low spirits?
Reginald: I don't know.
Bartholomew: A bluebird.

— & —

Bartholomew: What is the best way to make a fire with two sticks?
Reginald: Beats me.
Bartholomew: Make sure one of the sticks is a match.

Bartholomew: What do you drop when you use it and take back when you don't?

Reginald: I can't guess.

Bartholomew: An anchor.

—— & ——

Bartholomew: What are the three fastest means of communication?

Reginald: I have no idea.

Bartholomew: Telephone, telegraph, and tell-a-secret.

—— & ——

Bartholomew: What is good advice for a young baseball player?

Reginald: You tell me.

Bartholomew: If you don't succeed at first, try second base.

—— & ——

Bartholomew: What is a fast duck?

Reginald: I give up.

Bartholomew: A quick quack.

—— & ——

Bartholomew: What happens when a chimney gets angry?

Reginald: Who knows.

Bartholomew: It blows its stack.

Bartholomew: What is the difference between a locomotive engineer and a schoolteacher?

Reginald: You've got me.

Bartholomew: One minds the train, while the other trains the mind.

—— & ——

Bartholomew: What state saved Noah and his family?

Reginald: My mind is a blank.

Bartholomew: Ark.

—— & ——

Bartholomew: What is the rudest bird?

Reginald: That's a mystery.

Bartholomew: The mockingbird.

—— & ——

Bartholomew: What has fingers and thumbs but no arms?

Reginald: I'm blank.

Bartholomew: Gloves.

—— & ——

Bartholomew: What is a good way to keep a dog off the street?

Reginald: I don't have the foggiest.

Bartholomew: Put him in a barking lot.

Bartholomew: What would you call your tailor if you forgot his name?

Reginald: Search me.

Bartholomew: Mr. So-and-So.

— & —

Bartholomew: What part of London is in China?

Reginald: You've got me guessing.

Bartholomew: The letter N.

— & —

Bartholomew: What is a cold war?

Reginald: I pass.

Bartholomew: A snowball fight.

47

What Do You Get When?

Q: What do you get when you cross a telephone and a pair of scissors?

A: Snippy answers.

— & —

Q: What do you get when you cross a cat and a pickle?

A: A picklepuss.

— & —

Q: What do you get when you cross quackers (crackers) and milk?

A: Ducks and cows?

Q: What do you get when you cross an owl and a goat?

A: A hootenanny.

Q: What do you get when you cross a lion and a mouse?

A: A mighty mouse.

48

Side Splitters

First jailbreaker: How did you get rid of the bloodhounds that were trailing us?

Second jailbreaker: I just threw a penny in the river and they followed the cent.

— & —

Q: Do ships like the *Titanic* sink very often?

A: No, only once.

— & —

Oscar: Your sister is spoiled, isn't she?

Jerome: No, that's just the perfume she's wearing.

— & —

Father: Son, what did you learn in school today?

Son: I learned that all those math examples you did for me were wrong.

Hubert: This match won't light.
Gilbert: What's the matter with it?
Hubert: I don't know. It worked a minute ago.

—— & ——

I don't want to say I am a bad baseball player, but usually they put the worst player in right field. The last time I played with the team, they put me in Indiana.

—— & ——

Policeman: When I saw you driving down the road, I thought to myself, "Sixty-five at least."
Woman driver: I don't think that is quite fair. I think this hat makes me look older.

—— & ——

Edgar: Have you ever studied a blotter before?
Wade: No, why?
Edgar: You should try it. It's very absorbing.

—— & ——

Q: What school do you have to drop out of in order to graduate?
A: Parachute school.

—— & ——

Most people don't act stupid—with them it is the real thing.

Did you hear about the guy who baked a firecracker into his pancakes? He really blew his stack.

—— & ——

Q: Suppose there was a monkey in each corner of the room; a monkey sitting opposite each monkey; a monkey looking at each monkey; and a monkey sitting on each monkey's tail. How many monkeys would there be?

A: Only four monkeys. Each monkey was sitting on its own tail.

—— & ——

Willard: My hair is coming out. What can I get to keep it in?

Malcolm: Try a paper sack.

—— & ——

Ken: Did I ever tell you about the time I came face-to-face with a tiger?

David: No. What happened?

Ken: I did not have a gun. I just stood there. The tiger crept closer . . . and closer . . .

David: Gosh, what did you do?

Ken: I just moved on to the next cage.

—— & ——

Some men were discussing the Bible. They were wondering how many apples Adam and Eve ate in the Garden of Eden.

First man: I think there was only one apple in the Garden.

Second man: I think there were ten apples. Adam 8 and Eve ate 2.

Third man: I think there were sixteen apples. Eve 8 and Adam 8 also.

Fourth man: I think all three of you are wrong. If Eve 8 and Adam 82, that would be a total of 90 apples.

Fifth man: You guys don't know how to add at all. According to history, Eve 81 and Adam 82. That would be a total of 163 apples.

Sixth man: Wait a minute! If Eve 81 and Adam 812, that would make a total of 893 apples.

Seventh man: None of you guys understand the problem in the slightest. According to my figuring, if Eve 814 Adam and Adam 8124 Eve, that would be a total of 8,938 apples in the Garden. At that point all of the men gave up.

—— & ——

Barney: What do you get when you cross a rabbit with a spider?

Blanche: I give up, what?

Barney: A harenet.

—— & ——

Blowing your own horn only makes other people go deaf.

49

Elephants, Elephants, and More Elephants

Q: What's gray and stamps out jungle fires?
A: Smokey the Elephant!

— & —

Q: What time is it when an elephant sits on a fence?
A: Time to buy a new fence!

— & —

Q: Why did the elephant lie on his back in the water and stick his feet up?
A: So you could tell him from a bar of Ivory soap!

— & —

Q: Why do elephants have flat feet?
A: To stamp out burning ducks!

Q: How do elephants get in trees?.
A: They parachute from airplanes!

— & —

Q: Why do elephants have flat feet?
A: From jumping out of palm trees!

— & —

Q: What would you say if you saw nine elephants in green socks rolling down the street and one elephant wearing red socks rolling down the street?
A: Nine out of ten elephants wear green socks

— & —

Q: Why is an elephant gray, large, and wrinkled?
A: Because if he were small, white, and round, he would be an aspirin.

— & —

Q: Why are elephants so wrinkled?
A: Did you ever try to iron one?

— & —

Q: Why does an elephant have a trunk?
A: Because he'd look pretty silly with a glove compartment.

Q: Why is it dangerous to go into the jungle between two and four in the afternoon?

A: Because that's when elephants are jumping out of palm trees!

—— & ——

Q: Why are pygmies so small?

A: They went into the jungle between two and four in the afternoon!

—— & ——

Q: Why does an elephant wear sunglasses?

A: If you were the one they were telling all these jokes about, you would want to hide, too.

—— & ——

Q: Why did the elephant swim on his back?

A: So he wouldn't get his tennis shoes wet.

—— & ——

Q: Why is an elephant gray?

A: So you won't mistake him for a bluebird.

—— & ——

Q: What do you get when you cross a parrot with an elephant?

A: A ten-ton bird that eats peanuts.

Q: Why do elephants step on lily pads?
A: Because the water won't hold them up

— & —

Q: Who started all these crazy elephant jokes?
A: That's what the elephants would like to know.

50

Leftovers

Q: Which bird is always out of breath?
A: A puffin.

—— *&* ——

Q: What do they call a man who always finds things dull?
A: The scissor grinder man.

—— *&* ——

Pilot: Have you ever flown in a small plane before?
Passenger: No, I haven't.
Pilot: Well, here's some chewing gum. It will help to keep your ears from popping.
Pilot (after the plane landed): Did the gum help?
Passenger: Yep. It worked fine. The only trouble is I can't get the gum out of my ears.

Chuck: Isn't the plumber here yet? I've been plugging this leak with my finger for five hours.

Chester: Well, you might as well stop. The house is on fire.

— & —

Albert: I have a very smart dog. He is good in math.

Gilbert: Aw, I bet he isn't.

Albert: Watch. Fido, how much is 100 minus 100? Sure enough . . . Fido said nothing.

— & —

I don't want to say my friend is boring . . . but at parties he stays in the room with the coats. Sometimes a few of the coats even leave.

— & —

Q: What do you call someone who always tells you about the problems you are going to have in the future?

A: A misfortuneteller.

— & —

The best way to save face is to keep the bottom half shut.

Wife: Honey, I can't get the car started. I think it's flooded.

Husband: Where is it?

Wife: In the swimming pool.

Husband: It's flooded.

—— & ——

Cowhand: It looks like you are putting the saddle on backward.

Dude: A lot you know about it. You don't even know which way I am going.

—— & ——

Sunday school teacher: Malcolm, do you want to go to heaven?

Malcolm: I'd better not. My mother told me to come straight home after Sunday school.

—— & ——

Sergeant: Private, I think the enemy soldiers are hiding in the woods. I want you to go in there and flush them out for us.

Private: Okay, sir, but if you see a bunch of guys running out of the woods, don't shoot the one in front.

—— & ——

Did you hear about the teenager who went to the barbershop. He had long, flowing hair plastered above his ears. His hair glistened in the light. The barber asked him if he wanted a haircut or just an oil change.

Did you hear about the paratrooper who jumped out of the airplane without a parachute? He thought it was a practice jump.

—— & ——

Olive: Why does your dog keep turning around in circles?

Oscar: He's a watch dog and he's winding himself up.

Other Books by Bob Phillips

For information on how to purchase any of
the above books, contact your local bookstore
or send a self-addressed stamped envelope to:

Family Services
P.O. Box 9363
Fresno, California 93702